ellis mode

poems
harvey ellis

First Edition: 2023
Rs. 200/-

Cyberwit.net
HIG 45 Kaushambi Kunj, Kalindipuram
Allahabad - 211011 (U.P.) India
http://www.cyberwit.net
E-mail: info@cyberwit.net

Printed at Vcore.

Ellis Mode

always Joan . . .

time

is a long sentence
with many vowels

we flicker in
and out
like train lights passing

speak to me
of things that want
to be told

while there is time

Contents

Play is the highest form of research

—Albert Einstein

the embrace

the embrace
contained
my ancestors
and everything
about my past

as if the closure
of my arms
around her
was also an opening

as if the little cells
of happiness and pain
realized
their common beginnings

and released
the long distances

some partial
exhaustions
followed
uncovering the
little pleasures

who for an instant
even sang

and she said

the bird
flew directly
at her
and chirped
3 times

then flew into
the tree

what she meant to say
was that bird
carried some
of his spirit

and I wondered
what part of the soul
flies into a bird
and signals
the grieving
loved one
like that

I imagined
the color orange
shifting its weight
into the strings

and pulleys

that flapped the wings
until it made
its signal of goodbye

just a little trail
of I love you
in the ripple
it made
on the surface
of the air

not the flowers

not the flowers
but that
you brought them

standing
on my desk
like a fragrant
memory

the room acknowledges

and the air
commits all this
to memory

how clear
the sunlight
floating in
on the aroma
of freesias

I am suspended

as colors
untie the tension
in my mind

and the moment
holds itself upright
as the flowers
try hard not to wilt

her kiss

what surprised
the kiss
was how easily
it landed

as if it had
practiced
itself
in secret

something unfrozen
relaxed the room
now that
the message
was given

he could feel
the tension
wash away like rain

and his questions
answered
before he knew
he had them

this and that

truth was interested
in what fiction thought
while fiction
didn't care

both were true
only one
made a big deal
out of it

fear

it comes
sometimes
as a mirror
of two things

a tunnel
darkening

and a stairway
that gets
brighter

as if the problem
of fear
is also a promise
of resolution

the man on the stair
turning
to look back

his face
covered
in darkness

the door

the door
to nowhere
was easy to open
but gave no reason to

except

insofar as doors
like to swing
on their hinges
letting in light

and shadows
of things which
could not otherwise
be seen

this one
was on the edge
of a silly hill
which had no reason
to be there

except

to hold a door
in a fence
so that someone

could speculate
on doors

and their preferences

and what pleasures
they give
when asked

stillness

some silences
have no solution
but for the way doors
have to have door wells
to open
into the next path

the rise in the road
flattens
and the birds have quieted
their song
only the window curtain
moves
in the shifting air

this would be a scene
not of your own making
but something
to pass through
without walking

time
like the weight
of heavy clothes

morning
grinding into view

what's not of interest

what's not
of interest
scratches at
my door
trying to get
interesting

like the run
back to Safeway
for the credit card
I thought I left
but found
out of place
in my billfold

you see
that uninteresting fact
just made it
in the door

some of us 40 years later

are busy thinking
we are the same

some busy
being dead

their absences
glowing
like little surprises
that tried
to tell us something

things change
then they remind you
they've changed

all this regret
and all this pleasure
sliding in and out
of the decisions
we've made

unbidden

dreams come unbidden
across a granary floor

they rattle
among themselves
like gossip clowns

they steal
from memory
and from each other
with no apology

they are immortal

after you die
still talking
indiscriminately
to anyone
who will listen

touching her

touching her
just there
like sunlight
on the back
of a maple leaf
gave the same
warmth
as if the hand
could contain
light

she was distracted
into the pleasure
of it
just like there were no
inhibitions
to worry about

how rich
she thought

how lucky
he thought

for Eric

not just your stories
but the way
you told them

I could have listened
to a tree stump
if you were the voice
telling

but now your bottled up
life
is waiting to be heard
before it closes in darkness

what you tell
I will tell

in that way
we penetrate the dark
with the little laughters

how form organizes thought

what the paragraph
does
is force thought

away from
the addiction
of run on

said is said
repeating just flogs
the idea

let it do its work
like a boat
set on water

at peace
with the movement
of the tides

self-assessment

measuring
your own hard on
in the mirror
there will always be
exaggerations

accuracy
in this case
only to the level
of the ego's
frustration

science
goes so far
and then
there is
personality

not how long
your dick is
as they say
but how
you use it

pixels

if my photo
is compressed
what does that do
to me

have I lost
something
between the pixels

a kidney
a memory
about dancing
with Janet
in the living room
with the furniture
pushed back

representations
and the self
are cousins
that speak
to each other

I wanted
a photo
what I got
was questions

stuck in my head

so where
does that music play
from
that song that's waiting there
like a sidebar
when I wake up

plowing along
like an atomic clock
not listened

my inside ears
turn away
and come back
and still it's there
plugging away
like a compulsion
that clicks in
when you walk
counting squares
on the sidewalk

what hearing
got this all started

forgotten
as the consonant
at the beginning
of a sentence

a beam of light
who's lost
its source

and still shining

toasted

at the reunion
some of the faces
were the same

just toasted
a little
in the oven of time

some hardly
recognizable

body weight
uniformly
bloat

opinions sharp
as shattered
sugar cane

uncertainties
washed away

the little hatreds
scrubbed and polished

memory pockets
unbuttoned

summer

at solstice
more light
piles up in
our window
boxes
between 7 and 9
a.m.

more heat

even the cool night air
has a thermal
tone

dark is not so
dark
at either end
of night

but will stage
a comeback
starting about now

suddenly bare feet
suddenly
swimsuit immodesties

and girls on roller skates

if words

if words
lie in a pile
like pick up sticks

do their meanings
bleed into each other

does Hawthorne
become
a time zone

maybe envy
an ocean floor

we could make love
into a Breakfast
Special Delight

or war
into a lacy doily

hands joined
where they fall

power
sparking the tight junctions

enter and alter

the violence of light
in a dark room

the way it commands
what it touches

how music
arranges a space
for sound

and the power of thought
to capture
the forms of things
where they lie shapeless
in the cluttered rooms
of the imagination

I could have slept
all night
instead of thinking
about this but

the words grew
restless
where they jumbled together
down there
on the evening floor

and just had to fall
into this strange order
of their own making

little narrative

not the man
but the story
of the man
in her life

no small wonder
how it replaced enough
of her loss
to provide a heart beat

and a metabolism
for her hungry body
all those years

until she finally
met the man

and
no longer needed
this story

levitation and matter

if I could levitate
it might be
easier
than walking
in the dark

what rooms
anyway
can exist
if we don't build
them so
outrageously

while we're
at it
why not
beam me up
Scottie

as if matter
could for 3 seconds
be antimatter
avoiding the need
for levitation
altogether

and then
change back

quicker
than a floating thought

leaving me
stumbling in the dark
practicing

cold hustle

nothing like
a little cold air
in the room
to hurry
the project

instead
of finding
a starting point
finding
your self
already started

it's a hesitation
versus
the work
of a chill's
desire
to creep across
your evening

little doubt
who won that one

naming the cats

she was surrounded
by acceptance
the way she
could even name
the cats
without objection

as if a
cool buttercream
atmosphere
had assembled
around her

in this manner
she could let flow
her personality
and choices
that had been
hiding
under the covers
all these years

he exchanged
any disagreement
he may have had for silence
and the release
of clingy responsibility

in that way
control relaxed
into danger

and the cats had names
he never
would have thought of

affair

her solution
to the problem
of her affair

was a threesome

the husband thus
had two astonishments
to deal with

and that
while opening
his bedroom
to a stranger

the ripples of this
extended widely
as the old life
no longer lived
outside memory

a new insanity
floated through
the rooms
inviting ideas

like why not a foursome
adding some
as yet to be determined

young woman
20 years his junior

he could see
the retribution
in that

he kind of liked it
as a price
of admission but

where would all this stop
if not
at the point
of refusal

which was fading quickly
down the road
behind him

her illness

her illness
becomes her

even as she
pushes it away
clinging
like a
sunburn
with its
own
timetable

they were distanced
by the space
between them
pulsing in the
night like
unanswered
questions

he sleeps casually
as the hours
cling and release

cling and release

they talk of
everything

and nothing

and whisper
blessings
in the night

chemo

what went missing
was the spark

the lightbulb
grew dim
trying to save
the light

and she cloistered
in her room
and nursed the
disease of the treatment
she had been given

as if the penalty
of living
required a little death
mixed in

the rooms
of her day lost
their music

and she staggered forward
against the tide
assaulted and weary

as sleep crawled
into her with

its large wings
of darkness

how absurd
she thought
that the will to live
requires so much
dying

and the writing

uncovered what was
under ground
writhing and squirming
like a landed gar

especially what she
didn't know about

as if a melon
shred open
simply by putting
words on the page

the words
sizzled in the
sunshine like
a melted witch

but the meaning
was not lost

the experience
was like
fingernails
on a rusty pipe

even so

she was grateful

for this new sense
of contentment
she could not explain

my parent's grave

I waited for messages
but found none

and the wind hovered
at the edge of the yard

like a homeward surge
missing something

my hard listening asked me
what have I

missed but the missed
stayed out there with the wind

and told me nothing
waiting patiently there

as stories
in unread books

I was in no hurry
having come miles

and years
to this place

where I could stop
and listen which was

it turned out
the blessing itself

the cherry tree

some subjects
want attention
like rainwater

others
rather smolder
quietly

the turn
of the day
slants a little
as we have heard
it will do

and leaves a kink
in the fabric
of our happiness

here the subject
is trying to create
its own attention yet

what cherry tree
doesn't have
off seasons

and still remember
how to fruit

resonance

he said to begin
a sentence
when the mind
is connected
to all its selves

brings
a horsepower
of cracking
activity

check out
my verbs
he said
my electro static
associations

abstract me
into my own
thought cloud
and bring me back
by the end
of the sentence

she
was not impressed

but my generators
are going
he said she said

she couldn't hear
the whine
of his turbines
having eaten soup
of a different
wave length

ahh resonance
he said sadly
good if you
can find it

she said
just make a little sense

tongue memory

and a few sour grapes

I just struggled
with that name
again

you know the one
that's not easy
on the tongue

maybe it's the tongue's
fault poor
tongue memory

sliding
out of the mouth
like that

maybe I offended
the name once
by not remembering it

and now
it refuses to be
remembered

as if punishment
was having to work

hard to pull it up
from its hiding place

between words like
national debt
and attrition

words that don't deserve
to be remembered anyway

the strange behaviors of ideas

some ideas surface like
fishing corks
that bob and drift

or spread and cluster
as insects
on a table cloth

some sparkle
some glow with desire
some speak 3 languages

from a foreign shore
I like the slow ones arriving
as packages of gravity

in the evening mail
the manageable shapes
and the little surprises

you might need a pencil
and a dark room
to capture them

reminds me of growing up
scratching the darkness
for ideas

some came vital
some like fossils
all shape and no life

or maybe inside the geometry
another geometry
turning inside out

how these shapes
invent themselves
how they dance

the way it is sometimes

if you want to know something
get porous and wait
for the water rising

she walked in the door
but her promises
came in sideways

like the time the room
bent all tilty
and unpredictable

I was eating popcorn
trying to be porous
and hoping for rainstorms

what came
was a lot of thunder
and dry air

how sexy to be unsettled

what you want
is an idea
that cracks you open

a slit of light
between who you were
and today

let it come
simply
on the back of a song

let it screwdriver
in
like a new gospel

wholeness
as a concept asks
to be fractured

a rock unstable
on the side of a
volcano

a branching point
in the fork
of a road

disturbance not all bad
when it comes
in packages like these

your urgent call

you realize
we dropped our place
in the coffee line
to come here

all skuzzy
and caffeine poor

your message
turned itself inside
out
with effort
and with yearning

how can you not
respond
to something
like that

in our blood
there are grooves
for shapes like this

their landing spaces
deployed
their electrical codes
humming

tell me your news
your ancestral connection
your purple emotion

my ear
spins like a radar
net

my blood ready
to open
its grooves

food for thought

it's anonymous
she said
and tasted
the tips of her tines

we can after all
turn the conversation to food
most any time

but what
was the secret
she turned
from

all colorful
in its joker suit
what

raw emotion
was too raw to let
the naming
begin

*   *   *

anonymous
she said as if
absence
had more presence

than presence
itself

a name floating
in the dark
all filled
with longing

I'm into
the what if category
she said
spinning possibility
like a deck
of cards

some uncertainties
are static
some Newtonian

and I wondered
if nonsense
were that self conscious

the way
you might sometimes ask
what the hell
was that

and not expect an answer
you could bring home
to mother

tuning

it's so late
at night
that I hear voices
in the fan

it tried to mean something
it really did

but the language
was just too electronic

maybe they said
my ear wasn't tuned right

the thief

want to help
fill my bank

any amount
will do

non-believer
that was me

got hurt

prayed a bit

and Mary
filled the room

I have my god
I have my gun

both comfort me
in their own sweet way

dystropic

she got icky
when she went
2 minutes into shrieky

little explosions
from under the liver
puking forth

I thought of horror
movies
how believable they have become
just now

anyway
a compromise
arrived like
the 11 o' clock
train

and our little
crack up doll
was herself again

and we all went off to dinner
without a whisper
of own it

filter

the star
through a curtain
is still a star

even though
its light
is forced
through a tea strainer

when the photons
leave the source
we've kinda lost control

but if I move my head
sideways
the light picks
a different part
to filter through

how important then
is my eye
to where the light
decides to go

I was thinking about this
until a cloud
came over

laptop and trees and the range of the imagination

the dream wondered
if trees growing
in my laptop
would mind
if the images kept changing

no it decided
roots and branches
don't have eyes

but the dream
remembered
that the message
lives underneath
the light
and the image

and then it wasn't so sure

but then the tree
spoke up

and said
it wanted to be transplanted

too many things
I said

too many wild things
to keep in mind

I closed the laptop
and went back to sleep

fractals

put on your magnifying glass
for the way
the shape spins down
to smaller iterations
of itself

it's a door that won't
hold still
showing up
after you've passed through
already

rocking out of the mist
like an imitation

shorelines that shape
themselves
from nothing

the janitor of the place
a shifty guy
flashes
vista points
like a maniac

pick a level he says
pick a level
and stay there

the detective

the detective
had a voice
like too many cigarettes
and too many
I don't cares

as if rough people
need to sound
like that

how about
a sleuth
called miss cream tonsils
and the revolver
in the library

maybe a death
strangler

its so unexpected

meanwhile this detective
grinds on
like a coffee mill
in a smoky room
and I

I do kinda know what
to expect

letter from Mars

on this windowsill
are the leftovers
of the future

forming themselves
in the predawn light

turning over and over
like a calculated risk

what scraps
tell about their source
is enough to keep
five detectives busy

what I need of knowledge
is not so specific

my compass needle
my wakefulness
and the shapes
that form the night
will do

as the line
between now and tomorrow
keeps changing

and leaving little scraps
for me to think about

Sunday morning

the bed
is not ready
to be left

a little rain wash
in the air

time
without schedule

and the body wants
nothing
but a little
absence of things

and yes

to be reminded
what it's like
lying next to you

severe beauty

while my body
goosepimples
over the swell of wind
outside

and the swirl
of branches

and the watery
currents
crisscrossing the night

my brain
is hoping
the playhouse
I built in the rain

has not hopped
down the street

severe beauty
has its downside

even so this chill
still sizzles me

tricky star

the star
at the edge
of branches
is watching me

how could
anything
peeking like that
not be

I took a deep breath
and it slipped
behind the next
camouflage
like it really
cared
about detection

or maybe
it's hiding from the wind
trying to blow it
out of the sky

it won't say
that it's planning to slip away
into the plasma
of a spreading
universe

why should it

lifetimes
pass before that
little transaction
takes place

meanwhile
the water
in the pot on the stove
might boil
if I just stop worrying

about things
like that

body wisdom

the thought came
that I'm about empty
of thought

but then vacuums
have a bad habit
of filling

so I listen
for the next rain storm
and occasionally

shift my feet
just to keep moving
and it seems

the body
keeps on thinking
whether I do or not

like the time this woman
saw her dermatologist
but the

in the body game
was not the outside
the body game

so she couldn't tell her
doctor about the little
coworker lustings

or the time
her father spanked
her

it was the difference
between taking a bath
and eating a meal

just a little surface game
when the body
has its own plan

so she left her secrets
with the hairdresser

reunion

the emails
went back 40 years then
came back
to the return address

scooping up
history
like so much ice cream
all rich
and melty

so much space
in those four years
we occupied

and then suddenly
everybody
went off diverging

lines spreading out
which were
the rest of our lives forming

how could we know
how much distance
that made

memory fading
like we never thought
it would

my guess

she would pick up
on the intensity
of his wanting
her so bad

probably
she would let it all fall
to the side

like a conversation
that slightly
missed the mark

all this while he
saw little
openings

which later
proved artificial
predictable

isn't it
the way things flow
off course

while desire
waits like a crouched cat
with nowhere to spring

day zone

the day wants
to start
like a calliope
firing up

I swing back
to the roots
of night where they
still cling
to my forward motion

I am a phrase
reluctantly turning

a man with a song
in two rooms

a moon
drifting
into sunlight

daylight savings

somebody's
screwing around
with the hours
again

3 o' clock is 4
and the body
is asked
to tell itself
little lies

mostly
it's about getting up
earlier
like coal miners
and paperboys

I've been a paperboy
I am done
with that

but this new layer
on the clock face
has different numbers

and it doesn't care
what I'm used to

so I guess
I'll just shift my appointments
one hour later

the power of ideas

she had fun saying
she would give him
anything
he wanted

and feeling the power
of that idea
surge through
them both

as if each item
she mentioned
was a threat
of pleasure

an article
of clothing removed
item
by item

in that way less
was larger

even if it was only
the idea of it

*   *   *

but the idea
of breaking taboo
excited her

what surprised her most
was that
as she touched herself
her voice became
like a child singing

as if to do it
for him
meant finding out more
about herself

so she described
what it felt like
to him

the pleasure

and the exploration

of a new way

of seeing things

as if the offering itself
was the key to the door

storm epiphany

the rain's leading edge
has sucked itself
back up into the clouds

it hovers there
like a water balloon
armed
and benevolent

in my bed
I drift as if
under the electrical
crescendo
that precedes
joy

my cells resonate
with mountains
and oceans and
remind themselves
what it is like
to come alive

breathe deeply
I said
descend
into bedsheets

the clock
stops ticking
for this

white space and the pen

I found myself
diving into the page
the whiteness surrounding me
like substance
slipping into fog

the message was
a dark sliver of wood
hidden somewhere

and the voice of the page
was a floating voice
that spoke without sound
even language
was not necessary

but the pen thought it
wanted words
so the ideas
got together and trickled
down the mountainside
in rivers and shapes
that looked like meaning

there was a window there
that opened
and closed
and that was when
the music started playing

and the soul
that had not spoken
about this
came forward and said
it wanted to deepen
it wanted
more room

nothing would do
but that

and the words were afraid
they might be shallow
so they tumbled
among atmospheres
they'd not tried before
and where they came together
randomly
the friction
spoke in a quality of language
that untangled
the fibers of my mind

and I saw the difference
between what I make
and what comes to me
dressed in rags
of grace

riding pathways
I've never traveled

rising like a new sun
in a room next door

and it said look
behind the dark splinter
behind the words
to where the heart sways

a private world
where the winds
of the little chemistries
pass sideways
through the chambers

language
can only imitate
what lives there

but the particles
contained in the bag
of my body had already
been arranged
in their webs of
instructed connection

even so
the voice said
even so rearrange
yourself
rearrange if you want to know
the truth

the problem with waking up in the night

is not sleeping
when what the body wants
is both

the stars roll by
like white marbles
and the night deepens
into itself

what happens to time then
depends on the attention
I give it
wrapped in enough stillness
to slow down

where is my yesterday
where tomorrow

can the dawn dawn
before it gets here

I wouldn't think
of these questions
but for the fact
that time that has stretched out far enough
to allow me

my surfaces getting all mixed up

the pleasure of that

I am porous to myself.